Self-Editing Your Novel

Self-Editing Your Novel

An editor's tips to make your work shine

Kathy Stewart

Self-**Editing Your Novel:** ***an editor's tips to make your work shine***

First published in 2014 by
Authors' Ally
www.authorsally.com
27 Wallaby Drive
Mudgeeraba, Qld, 4213
Australia

National Library of Australia Cataloguing-in-Publication entry:

Stewart, Kathy
Self- Editing Your Novel: an editor's tips to make your work shine

1st edition
ISBN: 978-0-9808153-7-5

Fiction –Technique. – Manuscripts – Editing

808.3

Cover design: Mala Baranove

About the Author

Kathy Stewart owns and runs an editing and appraisal service situated on the Gold Coast of Australia. She has always been passionate about writing and has worked as a professional editor since 2004. Many of the books she has worked on are now selling in bookstores and online and many others are in the pipeline. Her manuscripts, The Chameleon Factor and Race Against Time, were shortlisted and longlisted respectively for the 2010 Crime Writers Association Debut Dagger Award in the UK.

Contact Kathy at: kathystewart640@gmail.com

Other books by Kathy Stewart

Novel:

Chameleon

Short story collections:

Over to You

Star Turn and Other Stories

Contents

Introduction

This book is designed for those who are writing fiction, namely novels, but it could also be used as a guide for writers of short stories and even non-fiction.

Drawing on my years as a writer, a manuscript assessor and as an editor, I've put together a guide that should enable you to avoid the common pitfalls that might prevent your novel from reaching a wider audience.

I hope it will help you.

First Steps to Editing

So you've finished your first draft. Congratulations. Writing a full-length novel is a wonderful achievement. It takes time and commitment – often years out of your life spent huddled over a notebook or computer while others sleep or have fun. But writing your novel was fun, right? I hope so, because that's why we write.

I hate to tell you this, but your work has only just begun.

If you want to see your novel in print or as an ebook, there's still plenty to do. Of course, you could just send off or publish your first draft, but it's likely to fail, and you don't want that, do you? You wouldn't have spent so much time sweating over it if you were going to settle for second best.

So what do you do?

Scenes

The first thing you need to understand is that novels are made up of a series of scenes. It helps if you can picture your novel like a movie, where each scene portrays another part of the story. The scenes are then threaded together to form chapters, which in turn go together to form your novel.

A commercial length for a novel is 85,000 to 90,000 words. Young adult and romance or erotica are often only 50,000 words. Ebooks are turning this convention on its head, though, as they're often much shorter than this and can be as short as a few thousand words.

So, once you've finished your first draft, you need to take off your creative hat and put on an analytical hat. Keep your tasks manageable. Be methodical and disciplined.

First, read through your entire manuscript. It's a good idea to read it aloud as you'll pick up many faults this way.

As you're reading, look for any inconsistencies such as changes in description, problems with the sequence of events, dialogue that could be more consistent with a character's nature, etc, but don't make the changes at this stage.

Discipline yourself to mark where the problems are without fixing them. You'll go back later and make any changes to passages where, for instance, a character's voice or dialogue doesn't seem right, where there are changes in tense, or where the syntax of a sentence seems to jar.

Planning

If you didn't do much planning before writing, there are three things you need to do now:

- Write an outline
- Construct a timeline or timelines
- Draw maps of places, floor plans of houses etc.

Outline

Your outline forms the framework of your novel and is often an important tool when writing the first draft. However, if you're a person who prefers to write by the seat of your pants and you haven't worked from an outline, you will need to do one now. Your outline should be broken down into chapters and each chapter further broken down into each consecutive scene.

In your outline, you will need to note:

- Who is the point-of-view character in each scene, or who is the main character in each particular scene?

- Where is the scene set?
- What action takes place in the scene?
- What conflict takes place?
- Does this scene further or deny the protagonist's goal?
- Does this scene further or deny the antagonist's goal?

At the very least you'll need to have the main or point-of-view character in each scene, where the scene is set and what action takes place. You can draw up your outline in a spreadsheet like Excel or as a table with appropriate columns (see in the following example):

Scene	Protagonist	Setting	Action
51	Scott	River gorge	Scott is forced to abseil into the gorge to retrieve the suspected murder weapon.

You can also write out your outline in a series of dot points if that suits you better:

- *Scene 51 – Scott – Setting: River gorge. Action: Scott is forced to abseil into the gorge to retrieve the suspected murder weapon.*

A number of programs offer software that will be suitable to draw up these outlines too, so if you'd prefer to use one of them, maybe do a search online. I tried typing 'outlining a novel' into a search engine and came up with a host of online tools. There are too many to mention here, but if this is the way you'd prefer to go then I'm sure you'll find one to suit your needs.

Whatever method you choose, drawing up your outline will take some time but is a necessary part of the process, as it will tell you whether you have any unnecessary scenes, if the settings are repeated or if there is not much happening in a scene. A hint here is that if a scene seems flat or unexciting, if there is no conflict or tension in a scene then either spice it up or delete it.

While on the subject of outlines, you also need to decide:

The scene character's goal

In every scene, one of your characters will star. This 'star' does not necessarily need to be your protagonist (good guy or main character of your novel) or even your antagonist (bad guy or foe of your protagonist) but will most likely be one of them. So, you could extend your outline to incorporate a column marked 'goal' as well.

The goal in a scene should be tied to the overall plot in some way.

As an example, we'll use characters and scenes from my latest manuscript, *Clear Island Murder*, to illustrate some points.

Clear Island Murder is a crime story set on the Gold Coast of Australia. Scott Ryder and Kimberley Stanton are the two detectives who will try to solve the murder case. The book opens with Scott and Kim trying to rescue a recently released child murderer, Grant Lambert, and his elderly parents from an incensed mob. I've shortened the following extract, so please excuse the copious ellipses.

'Look at that idiot!' Detective Scott Ryder swung the wheel to avoid the cameraman. The headlights flashed a white beam across body and camera.

Scott glanced at his partner, Kimberley Stanton, who sat white-faced, jaw set, beside him.

Beyond the cameraman, a crowd milled. It had gathered quickly. That afternoon, Grant Edward Lambert, wrongly convicted child murderer, had been released from prison, and no one should know where he was staying. The news had leaked out. It was a mark of their fervour that they were here at 2am, when most folks should be in bed.

How would Kim react in this situation? Had she dealt with mobs? He had no idea. He had only known her three weeks. He hardly knew her or the Gold Coast. But mobs were familiar to him. He'd dealt with plenty of those in his previous law enforcement career before arriving in Australia.

'Stephen Ridley's here. I should have known.' Kim's voice sounded bitter.

'Who is he?'

Kim indicated. 'That TV reporter. He had his moment in the limelight twelve years ago during the original Grant Lambert case. Now he's determined to have it again.'

Scott's gaze followed the direction of his partner's glare. Sure enough, centre stage amongst the angry mob was the reporter, microphone in hand, the light of the TV camera focused on his animated face. Around him and to one side swarmed the crews of rival television stations.

Blue and red lights from the police cars already at the scene reflected off the wet tarmac. A flash of lightning followed by a rumble of thunder from the retreating storm lit up faces in the crowd. Men and women, their ranks swelled by late-night revellers drawn to the action, held impromptu placards, mouths contorted in anger as they spewed their vitriol towards the high-set old Queenslander where Grant Edward Lambert was holed up with his elderly parents.

Scott parked the car away from the crowd and strode towards the uniformed policemen trying to hold the crowd at bay. The din assaulted his eardrums. Words of hate built to a crescendo as chants of 'Die, Lambert, die' reverberated off walls and dissipated into the darkness.

'Can you hold them?' Scott shouted to a thickset cop with black hair.

'For now. But I'm not sure for how long. We need the Lamberts out of there. If this mob breaks free, they'll kill them. And that bastard Ridley's doing nothing to help.'

The TV reporter's face shone with sweat. His voice could be heard through the chants...

Scott turned on his heel and met Kim halfway to the police cars.

'Lock him up!' someone yelled.

'Why'd you set him free?'

'Protect our kids!'

Scott kept his gaze resolute as he strode back to the car. Kim slid in beside him. 'Can you get the Lamberts' phone number?' he said to her. 'We need to find out how they're doing and the lay of the land. If there's a way out the back, they should know it.'

... In under a minute, they had the number. Scott pulled out his phone and dialled ... The noise of the crowd increased ... A trembling voice answered.

'Mr Lambert? Detective Scott Ryder here ... We're here to get you out of there.' He paused to allow the elderly man to assimilate his words and then continued firmly but gently ... 'Is there any way out of the yard, perhaps into the neighbour's yard at the rear or onto that walkway?'

He could hear the noise outside the house transmitted down the line, an echo of the noise that made it almost impossible to follow what Ted Lambert said.

As Ted spoke, his voice wavered.

Scott could feel his terror.

When the old man had finished speaking, Scott hung up and turned to Kim. 'Right. There is a way out.' He pointed to the satellite map. 'We need to get to this road at the back, next to the park that leads down to the river.'

As we can see, in scene one Scott's goal is to save the Lamberts from the murderous mob, but he also has secondary goals such as doing his job well and learning to get along with his new work partner, Kim.

Kim's goals might be the same as Scott's to an extent, that is, she also wants to rescue the Lamberts from the mob, but she is more focused on Ridley and appears to hold him in contempt, as do the other police, who are more familiar with him.

Stephen Ridley, the TV reporter, is trying to heighten the tension; he is after a good story and if doing this lands the Lamberts in more trouble, all the better for him.

As you can see, Stephen Ridley's actions create conflict for Scott and Kim; his actions are diametrically opposed to what they are trying to achieve. Their goals are in conflict. Also, even though Scott and Kim are meant to be work partners, their differing backgrounds could add tension to their partnership. Scott is a foreigner in a foreign land; Kim is a homegrown girl and may not understand his unfamiliar ways.

What obstacles are there?

If the main character in any scene does not encounter any problems during that scene, there probably isn't much point in it being there.

To quote the previous example, Scott is trying to rescue the Lamberts from a mob who are intent on killing them. Stephen Ridley doesn't feel convicted child murderer Grant Lambert should have been freed from prison so he is intent on stirring up the crowd; he doesn't think beyond his present intent to the larger implications his actions might have for Grant's elderly parents.

Stephen Ridley provides an obstacle to Scott achieving his goal, but there are other obstacles, such as the crowd, the topography and, later, a news helicopter.

Think up as many plausible obstacles as you can to heighten the tension in your scene.

What does your character do to achieve his goal?

An inert character is not very interesting so introduce action, no matter how slight, at the earliest opportunity. If your scene starts with the character lying in bed, and then getting up to walk down the street, rather start with the character walking down the street. But don't stop there. Have something happen to that character as he walks, or have him stopped in some way, perhaps by a gunshot or by witnessing an occurrence that forces him onto another path, anything that will keep you character moving and your reader intrigued.

To quote from *Clear Island Murder* again:

A trickle of sweat ran down Scott's back as they emerged from the car and jogged across a well-cut lawn to a fence at the back ...

The noise from the street at the front had intensified, the chants coming thick and fast now. A helicopter clattered overhead ...

'Who's there?' Ted Lambert's tremulous voice came from the other side of the door ...

A moment's hesitation, then the click of a latch and the door opened a crack. No chain, Scott noted ...

Two people stood huddled against the back wall of the lounge, blinking in the dim light.

Scott recognised Grant Lambert immediately: the lopsided face, one eye larger and higher than the other, the small pinched mouth with lips that drooped on one side, giving him the look that had helped convict him. A prime candidate for 'monster', Scott thought ...

Marilyn Lambert's face was streaked with tears. Her eyes were round and wide behind her glasses, her face pale in the filtered light.

A loud crack shattered the window.

Shards of glass showered the room as a brick thudded onto the floor. Marilyn screamed and covered her head with her hands. The noise from outside was louder now, closer, as though the crowd was right there with them, screaming abuse into their ears. Scott could sense their vulnerability, as though the shattering of the fragile glass had removed the last barrier protecting them from the crowd.

Through the fluttering curtain, Scott saw two thugs challenging the police cordon, waving what looked like iron bars. A policeman ducked and in a flash the hoodlums were through, storming towards where the hole in the window had appeared, brandishing their iron bars, mouths twisted in angry abuse. Scott saw the wide-open mouths of the police officers as they pursued the pair but he needed no second bidding. With the line breached, there was no guarantee of the trio's safety.

'Quick. This way.'

Scott and Kim shepherded the Lamberts into the passage.

'You have blankets?' Scott said.

Marilyn blinked at him.

'Yes.' Grant's voice was raspy and hushed. 'In here.' He opened a door.

Scott shone his torch, the narrow beam concealed from the road. Without a word, Grant crossed to a bed, hauling a cover and thin blanket into his arms.

'Good. When we're at the door, cover your heads.'

... Ted Lambert's hands trembled as he fumbled a key from the rack near the kitchen door. Scott led the way down the rear stairs.

The yard remained empty and silent, in stark contrast to the chants and yelling from the street. Ridley's voice carried clearly as the helicopter whap-whapped away.

'Probably gone to refuel. Now's our chance.' Scott raised his voice to be heard. 'Can you show us the gate?'

Ted Lambert nodded and led the way to the corner of the yard. There, he ... lined the key up with the lock. Scott held the torch for him. Ted's hand shook visibly and he dropped the key to the ground.

'Let me.' Scott bent down to search. One minute. Two. The helicopter would be back. Anybody could realise the house bordered a park. If they did ...

Scott's hand grasped the key.

He inserted it and gave it a twist. Nothing. Terrific! Ted Lambert breathed garlic in his ear. Scott jiggled the key, exerted more force. It turned.

Letting out a breath, he pushed the gate open and surveyed the darkened pathway. At the end that spilled onto the street at the front of the house, he could see light and the back of one car. If they were quick, no one would see them.

With the Lamberts concealed under blankets, Kim led them down the path to the car. Marilyn and Ted walked slowly, lifting the blankets with their hands so they could see their feet. Grant was right behind them, his gaze focused forward, his nervousness only betrayed in his jerky walk and the way his hands hovered behind his parents as if egging them on. Scott followed, glancing back once or twice to check no one had seen them.

From this we can see that Scott tries everything he can to rescue the Lamberts from their besieged house. He finds out about the topography, he manages to enter the house and then leads them to safety. The point is: he does something; he is not inactive.

How does his opponent try to block him?

This ties in to some extent to what obstacles are in the way of your character achieving his goal, but entails some intervention by your antagonist.

So if you have a strong antagonist, does he or she do something to block what your main character is trying to achieve? If none of your scenes contains this element then your antagonist is not strong enough and your conflict is not deep enough.

Besides obstacles provided by human antagonists, other obstacles could be the weather, the layout of a building, an act of nature such as an earthquake or a volcanic eruption, or the political situation.

If your antagonist is something non-human, such as the weather, or one of those mentioned above, then consider how you can worsen the situation for your protagonist by introducing a snowstorm, a cyclone, a tornado, or some other event that will raise the stakes inexorably.

Each scene should contain some obstacle your characters need to overcome.

How is the scene resolved?

In many cases, a scene should be resolved by landing the protagonist in deeper trouble. If your scenes end with all problems sorted out, especially early on in the novel, then you probably don't have enough conflict.

If you can make your characters really suffer on the way to achieving or not achieving their goals then all the better. Put them in hot water and then turn up the heat.

So, if your character is running away from a maddened gunman, have him trip and fall, maybe landing in a quagmire from which there appears to be no escape rather than have him simply find shelter. Think of ways in which you can heighten the tension at every opportunity.

Is there any striking imagery?

While it might be tempting to use all your best descriptive powers in every scene, sometimes this can translate to what is called 'purple prose'. Purple prose is excessively flowery language that can border on the ridiculous when overdone. You don't want to use purple prose because it distracts from the story you're trying to tell, but you do want to use at least one or two remarkable images that will have your reader gasping. These must be in context, of course.

While going through your scenes, check that you have one or two striking images that really bring your story to life.

Are there any surprises?

Nothing will kill the suspense in your novel quicker than having a thoroughly predictable plot. While readers will want you to meet their expectations in any particular genre, they also want to be surprised.

So think about what would be the likely scenario for any given scene and then check to see whether you have confounded these expectations in at least a few instances.

If you don't already have them, introduce some twists that break the expected. Once again, these can't be random surprises; they must fit in with your plot and be logical, but having some unexpected twists and turns will keep your reader reading.

Are there any interesting facts?

Modern readers are very discerning and in a brief survey I did of why people read and what they enjoy, one of the intriguing results to emerge was that readers like to be informed, be mentally stimulated and have their lives and knowledge enriched through what they read. By the time they finish a book they want to have learnt something they didn't know before.

This doesn't mean that you should incorporate huge chunks of scientific facts into your story, but rather that you should try to incorporate some interesting premise, fact or theory into your book that will educate, enlighten and stimulate imagination.

This 'fact' could even be made up but should at least seem plausible and be based on a credible-sounding theory. I'm thinking here of science fiction and fantasy, but the same principle could apply equally to a crime, thriller or mystery novel, or any of the other genres.

Examples of famous novels that have captured the imagination through using captivating premises or intriguing facts are the Leopold's Apple in Jo Nesbø's *The Leopard*, and the intrigue evoked by the facts revealed in Dan Brown's *The Da Vinci Code*.

Incorporating similar types of interesting facts into your novel will no doubt necessitate some research on your part but will undoubtedly enrich your story.

Are the readers' emotions engaged?

To fully engage your reader in your novel, you need to have emotional high points that make your reader feel. If you can make your reader laugh or cry, or feel anger or disappointment, or any of the vast range of human emotions that we experience every day, then you've done your job well. Does your scene make your reader feel some emotion? If not, perhaps the scene should not be there.

Ways to reveal the protagonist's true character more clearly

This point ties in with the character arc that will be described in more detail in the chapter on Character Development and refers to the changes that each of your characters will undergo during your novel. During the course of every scene in which they appear, your characters should be changed. That is, they will not be the same at the end of the scene as they are at the beginning. Are your characters changed by what has happened in this scene? If not, consider deleting it.

Ways to make the setting more original

Interesting settings make for more interesting reading, so rather than simply setting your story in a cafe or bar, perhaps consider using a castle or a bar in an exotic location, such as an island. In Jo Nesbø's novel, *The Leopard*, he uses a variety of settings in different countries from Hong Kong to Norway to Rwanda. Not only does he use different countries, he also uses intriguing settings within those countries, such as a house that has almost been consumed by lava, an illegal gambling den in the back room of a seedy restaurant, and a rustic hut in the snowy wilds of Norway.

Think of ways you can spice up the setting by adding twists or unusual characteristics that will fire your readers' imagination. Wring as much out of the setting as possible. That is not to say that you need to have long passages of description about your setting – quite the reverse – but you do need to choose an interesting and vivid location as the background for each scene. If the same setting features in too many of your scenes, consider how you can spice this up by changing the setting.

Timelines

This is a common problem with first-time novelists and can cause untold problems. If your timeline is not right it can affect your whole plot, as some scenarios just may not be feasible against a different timeline.

I edited one novel where the protagonist was born in 1900 and yet went to the Second World War in 1939 at the age of eighteen. As you can see, this is clearly not feasible – and no, it wasn't a mistake – the author didn't mean the First World War.

The problem was that the premise of this author's whole book relied on the protagonist being born some time before the First World War, so simply changing the birth date was not on the cards.

There were also problems with the micro timelines, and by that I mean the actions of the characters in their day-to-day lives or in their close one-on-one dealings.

For instance, you can't have a woman pregnant for longer than nine months, and you can't have a baby of six months able to run – unless your book is about some superhuman species, of course.

With that in mind, my advice to you is to do this critical step before you write your first draft, but if you haven't already done it you need to do it now.

You can have a number of different timelines. For example, you might need one for different years if your manuscript covers a long time span. You might need a timeline for shorter periods, for instance if there's a murder and the sequence of events for various characters is critical. So your timeline might span years, a week or a few days, but it could just as well span only a few minutes if the sequence of actions demands it.

The timeline can be done on an actual calendar. For my novel, *Chameleon*, which spans a number of decades between and including the First and Second World Wars, I downloaded calendars from 1914 through to 1946 and wrote against the squares what happened on what day.

The following calendar contains a timeline from *Chameleon.*

May 1946

S	M	T	W	T	F	S
			1	2	3	4
5	6	7	8	9	10	11 Catherine announces her engagement
12 Catherine has a confrontation with her family	13	14 Eve buys a car	15	16	17	18
19	20	21	22	23	24	25
26	27	28	29	30	31	

Your timeline can also be a straight line with incidents written along it. This example uses characters from the Scott Ryder series.

10.25 Kim arrives at the warehouse

10.25 Scott roars down the highway
knowing Kim is in danger

10.26 The door is ajar and there is no one around

10.26 Scott is delayed behind two huge trucks

10.27 As Kim approaches the door, a scream echoes
around the industrial complex;
she has no choice but to go in - alone

10.28 She enters the warehouse, gun drawn,
knowing Scott is on his way but unable to delay further

Or in dot points:

- 11 May 1946 – Catherine announces her engagement.
- 12 May 1946 – Catherine has a confrontation with her family.
- 14 May 1946 – Eve buys a car.

And:

- 10.25am – Kim arrives at the warehouse.
- 10.25am – Scott roars down the highway, knowing Kim is in danger.
- 10.26am – The door is ajar and there is no one around.
- 10.26am – Scott is delayed behind two huge trucks.
- 10.27am – As Kim approaches the door, a scream echoes around the industrial complex; she has no choice but to go in – alone.

- 10.28am – She enters the warehouse, gun drawn, knowing Scott is on his way but unable to delay further.

The advantage of this method is that you can add more points in convenient places, but if you use pencil to write on a calendar or to write out a linear timeline then you can also erase any entries which may not be correct and replace them as you work out the correct timeline. Or, if you have an image saved on your computer in a word-processing program you might be able to use the 'comment' tool under 'track changes' to insert your timeline. I managed to do this for *Chameleon.*

Maps

It’s essential to have floor plans of any houses used in your manuscript to make sure you can clearly envisage what happens where. If you don’t do this important step, you’ll find this disconnection between what you’re trying to convey through your characters’ actions and what the reader pictures is reflected in your writing. If you can’t picture a scene clearly then neither will your reader. Make sure you mark in where pieces of furniture are placed in the rooms and also any key features such as fireplaces, built-in wardrobes etc. A hint here is to base any buildings you use in your novel on structures you know.

You also need maps of places. Hand-drawn maps are fine, but if your story is set in the real world then you may prefer to use actual maps. Google Maps is great for this.

If your story is set a long time ago then try to find maps from that period or find photos or paintings which give you a clear idea of what the place looked like. For *Chameleon*, I was able to find maps of the country and even maps of the towns as they had been at the time in which the novel is set.

This point applies to non-fiction as well as fiction, especially if you're writing a biography or about some incident or person in history.

If you're writing fantasy or sci-fi then the world is your own creation, but you will still need a map. A hint with this genre is to base your world on some real-world place and alter it to suit your needs. This makes your job easier.

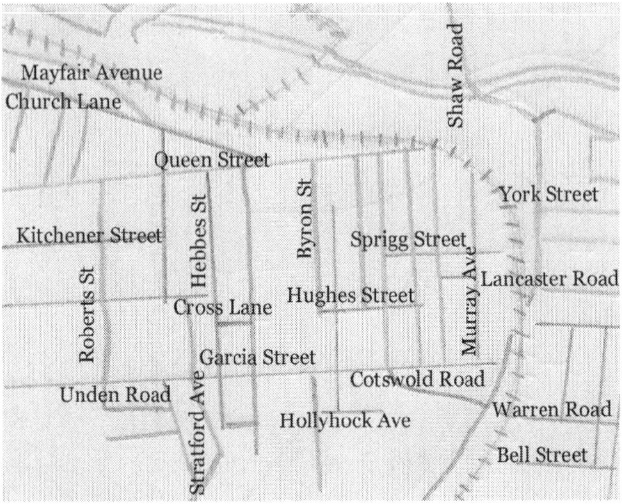
Mayfair Avenue
Church Lane
Shaw Road
Queen Street
York Street
Kitchener Street
Hebbes St
Byron St
Sprigg Street
Lancaster Road
Murray Ave
Roberts St
Cross Lane
Hughes Street
Garcia Street
Cotswold Road
Unden Road
Stratford Ave
Warren Road
Hollyhock Ave
Bell Street

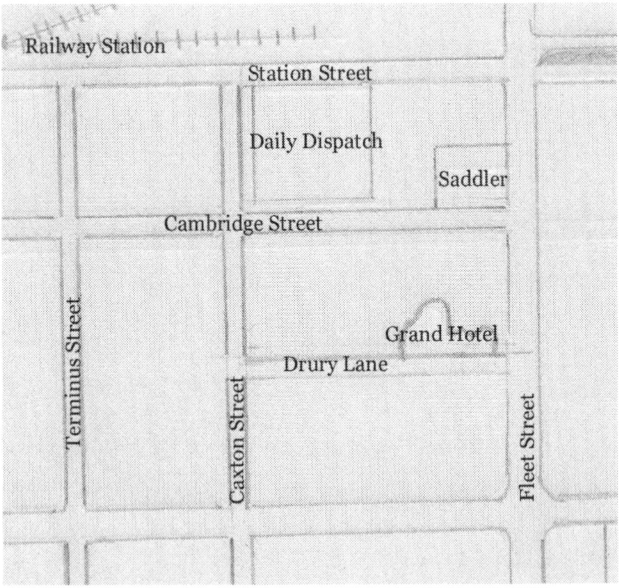
Railway Station
Station Street
Daily Dispatch
Saddler
Cambridge Street
Grand Hotel
Drury Lane
Terminus Street
Caxton Street
Fleet Street

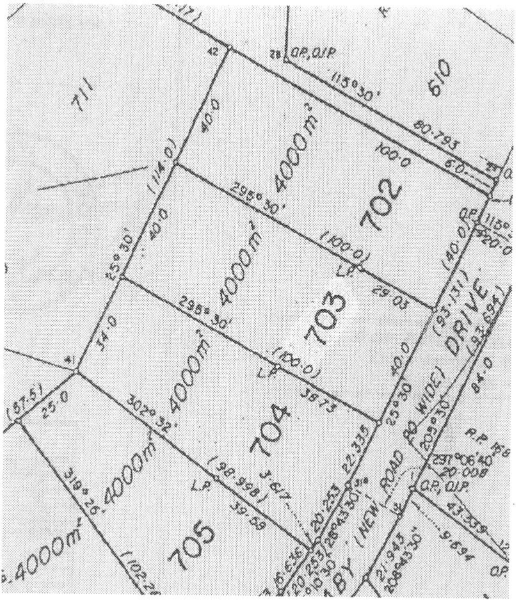
711
610
702
703
704
705
4000m²
DRIVE
O.P., O.I.P.

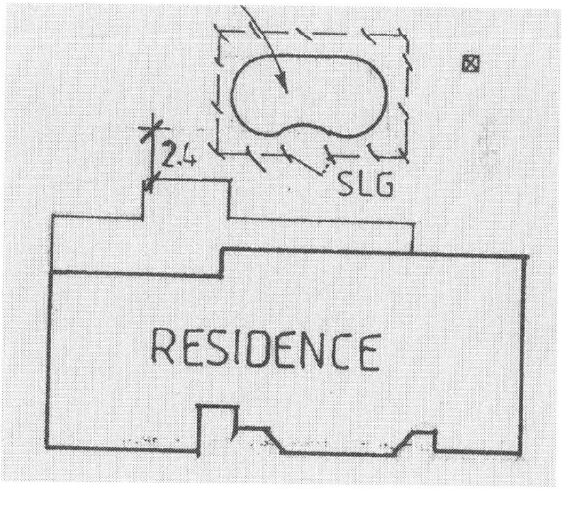
2.4
SLG
RESIDENCE

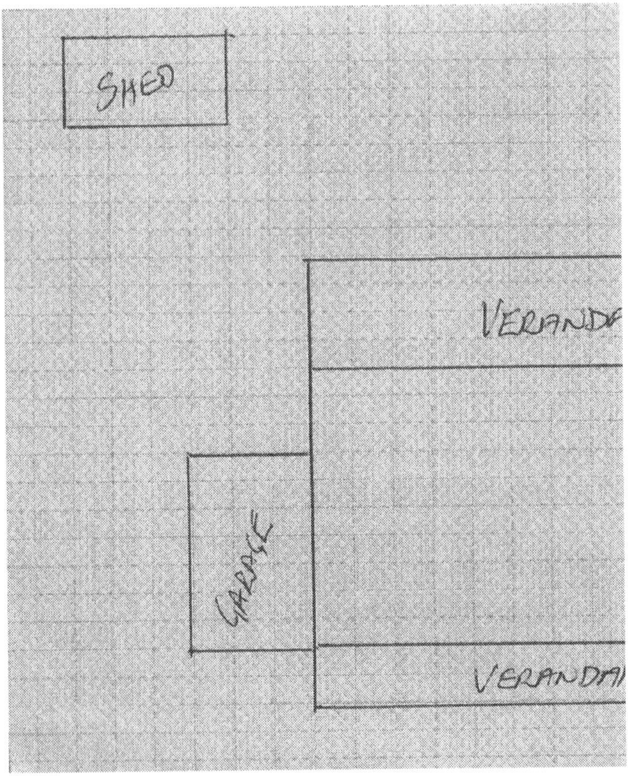
SHED
VERANDA
GARAGE
VERANDA

Tension and Suspense

If after examining your outline you decide that you need to add more tension and suspense, there are a number of ways you can do this.

Setting

Do you have long passages of description about your setting? If you do, this is something to look at. Long pieces of description can slow the pace of a novel considerably so it's a good idea to keep these sections to only a few lines in any one place.

However, as your setting can affect the mood of your novel so profoundly, my suggestion is to reserve some of your best writing for these descriptions. Choose your words carefully so that your images are powerful, giving your reader a wonderful sense of place in just a few lines.

Dialogue and action

Long tracts of narrative, describing setting and characters, can kill the pace of a novel. To heighten suspense, use action and dialogue to 'show' your story instead.

If you think about it, listening to a conversation or watching someone do something is far more interesting than watching that same person doing nothing while thinking. If you have a lot of scenes where your characters are merely sitting and thinking, then you need to consider how you can get them moving and talking. In fact, I would go so far as to say that if you have any scenes where your characters are merely sitting and thinking then you definitely need to get them moving and talking. But then I'm not a great fan of navel-gazing.

Narration

This follows on from the previous point about setting. If you have long passages of narration or summary, then consider cutting these down or eliminating them entirely. As before, a hint is to keep these sections to no more than a few lines in any one place, say three or four lines at a time. Another tip is to break up any of these segments with action and dialogue and then you won't go far wrong.

Thoughts or inner dialogue

At the risk of repeating myself, watching people sitting in a cafe absorbed in their own thoughts isn't anywhere near as interesting as listening to people talk or watching them do something, specially if the writer can make the readers 'feel' some sort of emotion too, such as anger, empathy or fear. If you can make pulses race and hearts thump as your readers run from danger along with your main character you have done your job well.

Long passages of introspection are common in literary fiction and also common in novels by first-time authors.

This doesn't mean that you can have no internal dialogue. As thoughts can be good to convey aspects of characters, and therefore help your reader identify with them, having some thoughts is often a good idea. Just don't have too much of this inner dialogue in total and definitely don't have a whole lot all in one place.

More about Outlines

Once you've been through your outline and decided which scenes you're going to retain, you now need to go through each scene to check whether you have included some important elements.

Create a hook

A 'hook' is a word, sentence, phrase or paragraph that immediately draws your reader into the story. This is particularly important at the start of your novel in your very first scene but it won't do any harm to examine each scene to see if you can start it in a better way. Don't overdo this or allow it to interrupt the flow of your story or it could become annoying. Some excellent examples of good hooks can be found in Ben Mezrich's book, *Sex on the Moon.*

Set the scene

This is often called 'orienting' a scene, or telling the reader where the action is taking place.

Soon after the start of your scene, ensure that you include a brief description of the setting, so if it's at a frozen lake, you could begin by describing your characters rubbing their hands together to warm them while watching two children skating on the ice. This often needs only one or two lines but straight away informs the reader where your characters are at that time. If you can, incorporate some sort of action and a 'hook' into this brief description of setting.

While your characters will then go on to do something even more interesting and speak about interesting things, you do need to throw in small clues at convenient places to remind your reader where this scene is happening. These small clues are called 'anchoring'. More about anchoring scenes later.

Have plenty of action in the scene

The key to any good novel is to keep the pace moving. If you think about it, which would draw your attention more: a person running down the street or someone sitting on a park bench? Clearly it would be the person who is actually doing something. You would immediately wonder about the person who is running. Who or what is he running from, where is he running to and why?

The action doesn't have to be violent. It can even be subtle, but the point is that action is more interesting than inaction, so make your characters do something, even if it's only to stand up and pour a cup of tea.

Use all five senses

Most good writers will do this automatically as it's part of the 'show don't tell' advice we are so often given, but it doesn't do any harm to check that you have done this correctly. A quick run through each page to make sure you have at least one of the senses per page will help your novel to come to life. While you're at it, make sure you don't use only one sense over and over again too.

For instance, if your hearing is not good, you may have omitted sound from your novel. If your character is unable to hear, this might be fine in his or her scenes, but make sure sound is included in the rest of the novel.

Dialogue

This won't always apply, but, generally, as soon as someone is talking your reader will find it more interesting. This also gives you the opportunity to show more about your characters by revealing their thoughts and beliefs.

They could be lying, which reveals a great deal about their character. The reader will ask: why is he lying?

The manner in which your character converses can also speak volumes. He may be hesitant or self-assured; he may have a good sense of humour. He could be angry, insane, have a warped view of the world. All these things can be revealed by what your characters say. Or by what your character thinks, in the case of an interior monologue.

Body language and gestures

This could just as easily be included under the heading of dialogue because body language can reveal volumes as well. Much of our communication is non-verbal. Some scientists claim that non-verbal communication is as high as 93 per cent, but most agree it can be as high as 60 or 70 per cent. Whatever the case, this is still a significant figure and as writers we can't afford to ignore this important part of our communication.

Allowing a reader to intuit what a character is thinking or feeling by interpreting their body language and gestures is a powerful way to make your characters more real to your reader.

If your reader is able to interpret clues about what the characters really feel rather than what they portray to the world, you will engage your readers more and they won't be able to put your book down. Readers love to identify with the feelings of your characters, so allow them to interpret the story in their own way.

Combine some of the elements

Making your words work harder by having them fulfil a number of functions can only improve your writing.

So, you could use a sentence containing body language to also convey information about the setting, particularly when you're trying to anchor a scene. For example, take this excerpt from *Clear Island Murder*:

Piper slammed his fist onto his desk, setting a cup and saucer rattling.

From this sentence, we know that Piper is frustrated or angry and that we're in an office where tea has been served in a rather formal way, that is, not in a disposable cup and not in a mug. So, in one sentence, we have sound, action, body language and setting. The words are working really hard.

How about this one taken from *Chameleon*:

Had I known it was an emissary of Milner's that was to be our guest, I would have taken more care with my dress. But, as it turned out, the envoy ignored me. I sat alone to one side, while they greeted one another with a formal handshake.

Oom Bart had polished his boots and leggings till they shone with an unaccustomed gleam. He held his hat in his large meaty hands now as he bowed his head to the envoy. They sat opposite one another, leaning forward, each with a brandy before him on the shiny round table. They spoke quietly, but with my sharp ears I could still hear.

The body language of Oom Bart and the thoughts of the narrator (Charlie) tell us a great deal. Oom Bart and Charlie need to be and are deferential to Milner's emissary. We can see this by the way they feel they should take care how they dress, by the handshake, the hat held in the hand, the bow of the head. The envoy feels superior: he ignores Charlie and focuses instead on the older man, Oom Bart. Oom Bart and the envoy are intent on something of common interest, which is possibly secretive, and they're drinking brandy in what may be a formal neutral setting, such as a hotel. Oom Bart is a big man, as evidenced by his 'large meaty hands'. Charlie is 'sharp', not only of hearing but also as regards observation.

See how much you can infer from such a short passage?

Anchor the scene at strategic points

This point could come under 'setting the scene', but it is a slightly different concept to 'orienting' a scene.

By anchoring, I mean strategically seeding sentences, clauses and phrases throughout a scene to remind the reader where the action is taking place. As mentioned before, if you can combine these with other elements, such as the senses, action, body language and gestures, your words are working harder and your writing will be more appealing.

Examples of anchoring, again taken from *Chameleon*, are:

'What it is?' Catherine's voice echoed off the cave walls.

And later:

Mandla stood a while, looking first from Catherine then to Eunice then out over the vista spreading below them. A sudden gust of wind swirled an eddy of dust across the slope directly below them. He turned to Catherine.

These sentences are used to break up the dialogue and remind the reader where the action is taking place, in this case in a cave high up on a barren mountainside.

Keep to one point of view throughout the scene

This is possibly the commonest mistake I see in fiction manuscripts and seems to be one of the hardest for most authors to grasp.

I must also emphasise that keeping to one point of view throughout a chapter or scene is a relatively modern phenomenon and certainly wasn't so strictly adhered to by many famous authors prior to about 2004. In fact I have noticed examples of point-of-view lapses in novels by some famous authors lately so perhaps this point is losing favour with publishers again. In case I'm mistaken, though, I do need to mention it.

To start at the beginning, there are actually three points of view you can use to write your novel:

First person: *As soon as I saw Oom Bart standing there, under the struggling gum tree, his hat in his hand, I knew there was trouble.*

Second person: *As soon as you saw Oom Bart standing there, under the struggling gum tree, his hat in his hand, you knew there was trouble.*

Third person: *As soon as he saw Oom Bart standing there, under the struggling gum tree, his hat in his hand, he knew there was trouble.*

Third person can just as well use 'she' or 'they' as the star, of course. The principle remains the same.

The most common point of view used to write a novel is the last one: third person. So the main character is referred to as 'he' or 'she'.

Not only are most novels written in the third person, they're also written in what is called the 'limited third person'. This means that the main character of any one chapter or scene cannot know what is in the thoughts of any of the other characters in that chapter or scene. He or she can only infer from their body language and actions what they are thinking, much as it is for us when we're involved in a conversation with another person. We can't know what they're thinking; we can only deduce.

To reiterate, writing in the limited third person has been in vogue for a number of years now, but that doesn't mean that you have to stick to these rules; all it means is that at the present time you'll find it easier to have your work mainstream-published if you conform. This fashion could change at any time, though.

So, the principle is to tell or 'show' your story through the eyes of one character only at any one time. This doesn't mean that you're restricted to one character for your entire novel, but simply that if you want to change who the point-of-view character is then you need to signal this change by starting a new scene or a new chapter.

This is actually simple to do and is often signalled by using a double space, an asterisk or line of asterisks or some other symbol to show the reader or editor that you know what limited third person point of view is.

A compelling story-line

There are some essential ingredients that go into writing a novel that will be a compelling read and it's a good idea at this stage to test whether what you have written will pass muster as a story that others will want to read.

The first thing to remember is that the driving force behind any story is conflict. Every scene that contains some sort of interaction between your characters should contain some sort of conflict. This doesn't mean that the conflict has to be overt or violent – it can be subtle – but it should be present even between friends and allies. The conflict should also relate to the overall plot in some way, which means it shouldn't just be random, coming out of left field, and it shouldn't degenerate into bickering. It should also be related to the scene characters' goals, either getting them closer to where they'd like to be or pushing them further from it.

The second thing is that the protagonist must want something desperately (for example, to survive or escape, win the contest or save the world). As soon as your main character takes action to achieve this goal, the story begins. But the opponent or antagonist will do anything to stop the protagonist, and their struggle needs to intensify all the way to the climax. Any scene that doesn't directly contribute to this struggle will come as an anti-climax.

Once the protagonist forms a goal, your readers begin to identify with her and worry about whether she can succeed. The more you reveal your protagonist's true character, the more strongly readers will identify. Character is revealed by the way she deals with adversity – the more pressure you put her under, the more she'll reveal her true self. So make her suffer!

Your readers won't be able to really engage with your protagonist unless you show her true feelings. Show her aspirations, her conflicts – both inner and outer – her fears, her dreads, and how they're evolving during the course of the story.

Suspense is a product of posing questions which remain unanswered for as long as possible – Can she survive? Will he win? – and it's the most important facet of storytelling, because it's what keeps your reader turning the page. If you can make your reader hope that your hero will succeed and be afraid that he might fail through creating more and more suspenseful situations all the way to the climax where the story is resolved for good or bad, then you've done your job well.

Pace how you reveal information too and by this I mean don't give away too much too soon. Withhold answers to questions for as long as you reasonably can so that your reader has to wait with anticipation for the solution to be revealed. This all helps create or increase suspense.

Unfortunately, most of us create characters that are very ordinary. While they might be realistic, in truth readers are more interested in characters who are bold, even bizarre, who are larger than life, with exaggerated characteristics that almost shout 'look at me' from the page.

They don't have to be particularly noisy characters, though they could be, but they do need to be people we would gravitate towards if they entered a room, characters whom we'd notice for some reason and be intrigued by.

Some memorable characters that come to mind are Lee Child's Jack Reacher and Jo Nesbø's Harry Hole.

Emotional highpoints

This point may not apply to every scene in your novel but does apply to your novel as a whole. Making your readers experience some sort of emotion at various stages helps them to identify with your characters more closely and also makes them care what happens to your characters.

So, while you're checking your outline and scenes, take some time to see whether you have included the following points:

Moral ambiguity:

Somewhere in your novel, at least one of your characters needs to face a difficult moral choice that will test them to the utmost. Their actions, either way, could make matters worse while trying to make matters better.

Betrayal:

We all know how terrible it can be when someone in whom we had placed great faith proves to be a turncoat or lets us down over a crucial issue. Is there a character in your novel who commits a betrayal so treacherous that it takes the readers' breath away?

Forgiveness:

Has one of your characters done something so dire, so awful that they need to be forgiven? It could be the betrayal mentioned above but could equally well be something separate involving a different character. Is there another character in your novel who is big-hearted enough or self-sacrificing enough to bestow that forgiveness? If not, it might be an idea to introduce this point to add to the emotional depths of your novel.

Change of attitude:

All your characters should be changed by the events that happen to them throughout the course of the novel, but is there someone whose life undergoes a radical change of direction, a shift so momentous that it almost amounts to a revelation? Is someone who has always felt one way forced by circumstance or by experiences to change what they have always believed to be true?

Sacrifice:

Does one of your characters have to sacrifice something they love dearly or maybe even sacrifice their own life or their career, reputation, job?

Unexpected demise:

Following on from the point above, is there a character in your novel that you and we love but who could unexpectedly and regrettably die? My thoughts here go immediately to Beth in Louisa May Alcott's *Little Women.* Try reading David Wroblewski's *The Story of Edgar Sawtelle* for one very fine example in modern fiction.

A good ending

The ending of your novel is an important part of your book as it will determine whether your reader then goes on to read other works you write. If you have a rushed or disappointing ending, your readers will be unlikely to read more of your work.

But having a good ending doesn't only apply to your novel as a whole. It also applies to each scene. While you are examining each scene, check to see that you have ended it in such a way that your reader is compelled to move on to the next scene to find out what happens next. Cliff-hangers can be a really effective way to do this, but be careful not to overdo these as too many one after the other can become annoying. Try to achieve an intriguing ending while still not overusing any one method.

A writer who is particularly good at creating intriguing endings is Ben Mezrich, author of *Sex on the Moon*, amongst others.

Character Development

Character consistency

Many writing teachers advocate having a folder for each of your characters or at the very least having cards or files in which you note essential details. Also, many books on writing contain lists of the type of character traits you need to know, which you can photocopy and then fill in. They're very detailed and you may feel you don't need to know so much detail about your characters, but the very least you need to know is what eye and hair colour your characters have.

But, to be honest, you also need to know their likes and dislikes, their habits, what job they do, what incidents occurred in their childhood, their fears, what sport they play, if they like music etc.

If you didn't draw up character profiles before you wrote your first draft then you need to do it now, otherwise you're likely to have a person's eye or hair colour change during the course of the novel.

You will also need to check that each character is unique. This applies to mannerisms, quirks of speech, dialogue etc. Perhaps go through each character's scenes to check that they have some traits that are unique to them.

For example, in *Chameleon*, I made sure that only Ellen used the word 'marvellous' to describe certain events.

Be aware of cultural and age differences too. A child would not speak the same way as an adult and vice versa, and someone who is not speaking in their native language might speak in a stilted manner.

Beware of using quirky ways to write accents, though, as these can be hard to sustain and even harder to keep consistent. Patterns of speech can effectively convey that a person is foreign, for example, without resorting to using odd spelling.

Character arcs

Each character should also have a journey throughout the story, or what is called a character arc. So they begin the story one way and are radically changed by the end of the novel.

You could draw up this arc for each character but it is essential to do so for your main characters.

So, in my latest manuscript, *Clear Island Murder*, Scott may start off as wounded, feeling strange and unsure but with very definite and hardline opinions about what is right and wrong. He is also courageous and determined.

Through events that happen to him in the book, he ends up less wounded, less strange in his surroundings, his hardline views have altered, but he remains courageous and determined.

The events in the book have had a profound and life-changing effect on him.

General Tips

Be consistent

One of the commonest mistakes I find in manuscripts is inconsistency, whether this be in spelling, or in descriptions of people and places. I'm going to assume that if you're reading this book your novel is written in English. The first thing to decide is which kind of English you are using. This may sound odd. English is English, right? Not so.

Strange as it may sound, we have a number of different types of English spellings for the same word and these vary from region to region.

The three I'm most familiar with are USA, UK and Australian spellings, so these are the ones I'll concentrate on. Please check a local dictionary if you are not sure which spelling is used in your country. I can't possibly mention all the variations between regions but listed below are a few common examples.

USA	**UK**	**Australia**
Harbor	harbour	harbour
Honor	honour	honour
Rumor	rumour	rumour
Realize	realize	realise
recognize	recognize	recognise
traveled	travelled	travelled
program	programme	program

As you can see from this, there are similarities and crossovers, but your readers will no doubt notice if you use honor in one place in your book and honour in another, or even honor in one place and harbour rather than harbor in another.

So, my advice is to be consistent in your spelling. If you're writing using USA spelling then keep it that way. If you're writing using Australian spelling, make sure you use this consistently.

Something to think about here is that the USA is a huge market for English-language books, so even if you live in another country you might like to consider using USA spelling. Just a thought.

There are other conundrums, such as, what's correct: focussed or focused? The answer is that they're both correct, but if you've used focused in one part of your book make sure you use this spelling consistently. The same applies to words like veranda and verandah. Both are correct but consistency in how you spell these words is the key.

Also, be consistent in what names you use and how you spell them. I edited one book where the female love interest was called Sahara in one place and then Sarah in another. And no, it wasn't a nickname for her. The author had just made a mistake. Likewise if you spell McCoy like this, don't suddenly change it to Mc Coy or MacCoy.

Another hint is to make sure that your names are distinct from one another. So don't use too many names that begin with the same letter or sound the same, because that's likely to confuse your readers and that's something you want to avoid.

If you find you have a Libby, Lucas and Lewis, maybe change two of them unless there is a good reason that their names should sound reasonably similar. Likewise if you have a Gary, Larry and Barry, consider changing two of these names to make your characters more distinctive.

When it comes to surnames, if your book is set in Scotland, for instance, don't have every Scottish surname starting with Mac or Mc. In this case you could use names like Campbell, Murray and Davidson.

Cutting Your Word Count

Most editors, agents and publishers see red flags as soon as they see a word count for a novel that exceeds 90,000 words. Of course, self-publishing and ebooks have turned this on its head, but it's still worth considering that if your word count is excessive you probably have a lot of words that could come out.

What's wrong with having a large word count?

A few things.

First, it's likely that you've waffled on about things that are not directly related to your story. Sorry to be so blunt, but it's most likely true.

Second, many readers are intimidated by the sight of a large thick book and it may put them off buying or reading your book, and that's not something you want to do.

Third, large books or heavy books cost more to post and this adds to the cost of buying a book so the expense may persuade a reader to buy a smaller and therefore cheaper book instead.

All of the above advice applies to print books. As mentioned near the beginning of this book, ebooks could make the last two points obsolete but won't affect the first point.

So, your word count is too long. What can you do?

There are a number of steps you can take and they're all likely to give you a crisper, cleaner story that will be more appealing to your readers, so don't feel that you're compromising by taking these steps.

With this in mind, consider cutting these:

Adverbs

Most adverbs are unnecessary in fiction, especially those ending with 'ly'. You could also do a search for each adverb ending in 'ly' to see if a weak verb plus an adverb could rather be replaced with a stronger verb. For example, *He walked quickly* could become *He strode*. Often, the adverb could simply be left out without detriment to the story.

Exclamations and curses

Exclamations and curses, while realistic, can become irritating and if you need to cut down on your word count see if you can dispense with these or at least minimise them. Examples are *Oh, God! Crikey! Damn!*

Adjectives

Writers often use two or three where one or none would be better. In fact, some books on writing teach that each adjective you add diminishes the one that has gone before rather than enhancing it. So instead of describing someone as tall and thin, you could simply call them lanky.

Words ending in 'ing':

Using too many words ending in 'ing' can become irritating, whcthcr they are used as parts of verbs or as nouns. So instead of saying *he was swimming*, use *he swam.* At times you won't be able to avoid using an 'ing' word, but it's worth examining each one to see if it could be replaced with something stronger.

Passive writing

Most writing teachers advocate that you should write only in the active voice, so what is it and what is the difference between active and passive voice?

Passive voice writing is often found in news articles and police reports and it can be useful in those cases.

It was reported that no progress had been made in the murder investigation.

If this sentence was rewritten in the active voice, it would read something like this:

The police spokesman reported no progress in the murder investigation.

A fair indication of whether you have used the passive voice is to look for words like 'was', 'were', 'by' and 'that'. If possible, do a search for these words and see if you can use stronger more effective verbs to replace 'was' and 'were'. Often, by rewording the sentence, you can eliminate these words and also 'that' and 'by'.

Here's another example of a sentence written in the passive voice.

The dog chased the ball that was thrown by the boy.

You could eliminate some words simply by rewriting this as:

The dog chased the ball thrown by the boy.

Better still, you could make it even more interesting by changing it to the active voice.

Lachlan tossed the ball and Buster charged after it.

Cut down or delete passagcs that havc too much description

As mentioned earlier, keep segments that describe characters or settings to no more than a few sentences in any one place.

Cut down or delete passages that describe characters' thoughts and feelings in too much detail

As with long sections that describe characters and settings, long passages of narrative or interior monologue can also become tedious. Cut these to only what is relevant to the story. And yes, you will need to be ruthless about this.

Cut out any repetition

This has to be one of the commonest mistakes I see in manuscripts. Please don't be tempted to reiterate facts that the reader already knows. I realise that a new character might not know all the facts, but rather than bore your reader with lots of repetition, use a simple summarising sentence instead, such as, *Scott filled Kim in on the details.* There is nothing more boring than having to listen to the same story over and over again. I can't repeat this often enough!

Cut out unnecessary backstory

Including backstory in a novel is always tricky. The author is often tempted to include more than is necessary. It's as well to remember that, while you need to know everything about your characters, not everything about their past needs to go into your book. A rule of thumb is that only those parts that have a direct bearing on the present story should be included.

Cut out speech tags

If you need to cut words an effective way to do this is by cutting out speech tags such as 'he said' or 'she said'. Use action to convey who is talking instead. Some examples of this are:

'Thank goodness you're back, Albert.' Martha straightened, hands rubbing the small of her back.

Or:

'Probably gone to refuel. Now's our chance.' Scott raised his voice to be heard.

Rather than:

'Thank goodness you're back, Albert,' Martha said as she straightened, hands rubbing the small of her back.

And:

'Probably gone to refuel. Now's our chance.' Scott said, raising his voice to be heard.

Cut out any 'filtered' thoughts

It's always best to avoid filtering any thoughts or feelings via your character. Instead, make sure you stay right in your character's head and write as if you are them.

So, don't say: *John thought she looked wonderful.*

Instead say: *She looks wonderful!*

Or: *Angie thought her mother looked angry.*

Instead: *Gee! Mom looks mad.*

As you can see, this is a powerful way to cut words from your story but it has the added benefit of making your writing more appealing by engaging your reader more.

Cut out certain words

The following is a list of words that can often be cut without affecting the story or character development:

About, actually, almost, appears, approximately, basically, close to, even, eventually, finally, just, just then, kind of, like, nearly, no, oh, practically, really, seems, simply, somehow, somewhat, sort of, suddenly, that, truly, utterly, very, was, well, were, yes.

Sometimes these words will be essential to the story but often they are not. Sometimes, instead of a character saying 'yes' or 'no' in dialogue they could simply nod or shake their head. At other times it will be essential to leave the 'yes' or 'no' in.

Dialogue can benefit enormously from cutting out words like oh, well, yes and no.

Conclusion

In conclusion, there are a few things to keep in mind as you self-edit your novel.

Read your work aloud as this helps you to pick up any inconsistencies in flow and dialogue, any awkward pieces that might need to be fixed.

Be methodical. Don't try to fix too many problems at once.

And be consistent in how you tackle the editing. Go through the process step by step so that you have a better chance of picking up any problems.

But most important of all, don't lose sight of why you wrote the book in first place. Enjoy the editing process, have fun, and then get on with writing the next one.

***

If you found this book helpful, please consider writing a review on the site where you bought it. Reviews are really helpful to authors and readers alike. If you feel like contacting me, please do.

My email address is

kathystewart640@gmail.com.

I'd love to hear from you.

9928714R00055

Printed in Great Britain
by Amazon.co.uk, Ltd.,
Marston Gate.